"Close to the Bone is a collection of delicious love poems that ignite every sense the reader has...deepening the ache within for the magical, tender kind of love there. During, between and around each line of lusciousness, I found myself wanting another poem, and wanting to be in the scenes myself. What a gorgeous tribute to intimacy and love."

~ *Laura Di Franco, Brave Healer and author or Warrior Love, a Journal to Inspire Your Fiercely Alive Whole Self*

"Erica's prolific creativity and bare honesty has produced another entertaining journey that tugs at the heartstrings of all who read her work. Equal parts mental evolution and emotional regression, it tells the fragmented tale of one person's trials when dealing with a lifetime of family, love, lust, self-awareness, and that sought-after quest for contentment in all forms...and the pitfalls that come with discovering exactly just what that subjectively means to each one of us. Each poem is different in pacing and rhythm, with a distinct feel that is the hallmark of Erica's signature style as a master wordsmith. This is a great sit-down read to witness one woman's empathy of the human condition in revealing her own experiences, as well as a great coffee table book wherein individual poems can be picked up at any time, even completely out of sequence. Collectively, they allow you to see how we may have different paths, but we're all really not that much different in our personal quests for happiness."

~ *Jason Salas, Author*

"Dorathina's visual depiction of a strong yet delicate female mind compliments Sand's effortless words. Each page is filled with a thoughtful sort of beauty — pulling readers in as they unravel the heart of each poem."

~ *Artemia Perez, local fine arts enthusiast*

"*Close To The Bone* is a thought-provoking literary mixture of introspection of the thoughts, and reminiscing upon the life, of its author Erica Sand. The beauty of her courageous vulnerability is easily felt in her poetry through which she uses her words as brush strokes to paint mental pictures depicting romantic, familial, and self love and the longing inherent in such human experiences. Her everpresent feminine grace is at times a subtle whisper, yet other times a passionate moan, but frequently yearning to fill and to be fulfilled. A few of my favorite pieces of Miss Sand's include her poems entitled "Plucking The Brow", "Translations", "Andu's Apples", "Sarah Means Princess", "Michigan Sandcastles", "Howl Poem", and "Spirit Within"."

~ *Rick S. Agustin*

"Sand's poetry is resplendent with emotive imagery. Both sensual and introspective, Sand's words offer readers a chance to share in her singular experiences. The accompanying illustrations capture parts of Sand's imagination and create springboards for readers' interpretations."

~ *Marie Perez, former lifestyle reporter*

# Close to the BONE

## Poetic moments of love and longing

### A Poetry Book

ERICA SAND

Copyright © 2017 Holly Rustick. All rights reserved.

Cover and Artwork by Dorathina Herrero

No part of this book may be reproduced, stored, or transmitted by any means - whether auditory, graphic, mechanical, or electronic - without written permission of the publisher and author, except in the case of brief excerpts used in critical articles and reviews.

Although the author and publisher have made every effort to ensure the information in this book is correct at the time of printing, the author and publisher do not assume and hereby disclaim any liability to any party for any loss, damage, or disruption caused by errors or omissions, whether such errors or omissions result from negligence, accident, or any other cause.

ISBN-10: 0-9989820-9-1
ISBN-13: 978-0-9989820-9-0

Discover other titles by Erica Sand at
http://www.ericasandauthor.com and http://www.sojourningsoulseries.com

*For my mother, Deborah Ellen,
for allowing me the gift of honesty.*

# About this book

This book is a compilation of poetry I have written over the previous twenty years. A small number of the poems have been published in a chapbook, Curvature (1999), a couple in The Grateful Bean Review (2000), and one in the Bamboo Ridge Press (2003), but most have been stuffed away in my drawers in old notebooks. I wanted to resurrect and officially publish these poems, as poetry has always been the deepest root of my love for writing and expression.

Grandfather's Tracks won the James Axley Award
in Creative Writing in 1999.

# PART I

*On romantic love merging into longing*

# Love Letter

I can only give you words.
As if they are something tangible you
can hold in the palm of your hand,
instead of just fluctuation
of soprano pitch.
As if these letters can be
unwrapped like a gift;
stretching out each letter
lengthwise to make a language
of infinite lines, stretching north and
south; suspended by
thoughts of you.

I can only give you an expression
of my thought process. Which
remains invisible like wind
until expression wins, and
jet streams shift.
The motion of the earth
tilted on this axis of 23 degrees

elicits my words that gravitate
towards you from this
latitude of 39 degrees.

I feel the weight of gravity, yet
I could be facing north or south
in this solar system as these
poles might as well be pushed light years
apart, never meeting in this parallel
universe; seemingly
suspended by thoughts.

But these words are given to you.
Stretched out from west to east, carried
across transatlantic jet streams
lengthened width-wise, alto tone;
makes me think of you and me
laying horizontally on a soft bed,
gravity pressing us magnetically together
as we tumble through this universe
unaware of which direction we are going;
suspended.

# The Space Between

I want to lie underneath
my man, look deep into
his honey-colored eyes, pour
myself into him.
The way he looks at me,
like some kind of wild animal,
as if we are not just surrounded
by the walls of his studio,
but by the universe,
the stars themselves.
His back arches deeply
and I can run my fingertips
across each and every muscle,
causing him to purr. Hair follicles
rise, nipples harden. And
our eyes magnetically connect
as if a nucleus is formed in
the space between and the peripheral
is just an outline of tissue.

Molecules exchanging and mingling:
a symbiotic relationship, creating
their own time. And I am lost inside
this space forgetting how long I have
been there, feeling the sweat drip
off his neck and onto my naked skin.
I feel myself let go and take him in,
become his prey underneath; solid.
A willing sacrifice or surrendered
Animal. I become his exhale, his
loneliness, his fear, and he is the Shaman
of this song. Because this is no
longer just a poem or an experience,
but has become dark matter — emptiness —
the only note. And our eyes still
magnetically connect
as if a nucleus is formed
in the space between.

# Nias

We spoke in yogic sentences, tainted by
your four-year malaria visitor, on a
hammock in Nias.
A double rainbow mirrored by a peach
sunset wasn't the only object reflected on
the second lunar eclipse in October.
Full moon in Nias orchestrated high tides
of talk of settling into houses nested in
New Zealand. All these omens
delivered an array of asanas on your bed —
in your sculpted arms by those five-foot
waves. Rising and falling
our moon salutation was
silhouetted by mosquito nets strewn
across the windows, the door, the bed,
tying up your old friend malaria.

# The Ritual Part A: Plucking the Brow

There is this way that the cup
of his palm touches my temples.

Curved over, he rounds
his muscular, naked back
and sits cross-legged like a
carved image of the
weeping Buddha.

With furrowed brow, he is
three inches away from me,
and inspects each follicle of
brow.

He takes tweezers,
and silver metal meets
coarse black hair.
Plucks one…hair
at… a… time.

This is a scarcity of his
meticulous side where
he notices black hair sprout
as if the tiny, ink-like hairs streak
his canvas.

Even though palm to forehead
is the only way our pores
migrate into one another, my entire
body becomes an extension of
this practice. He becomes
my guru, where I lay limp,
hypnotized with this change,
feel the evolution of my cells separate
with his pull. I am in his hands.

This has become our mantra
the staccato pinching of tweezers.
Are we even this intimate
when we make love?

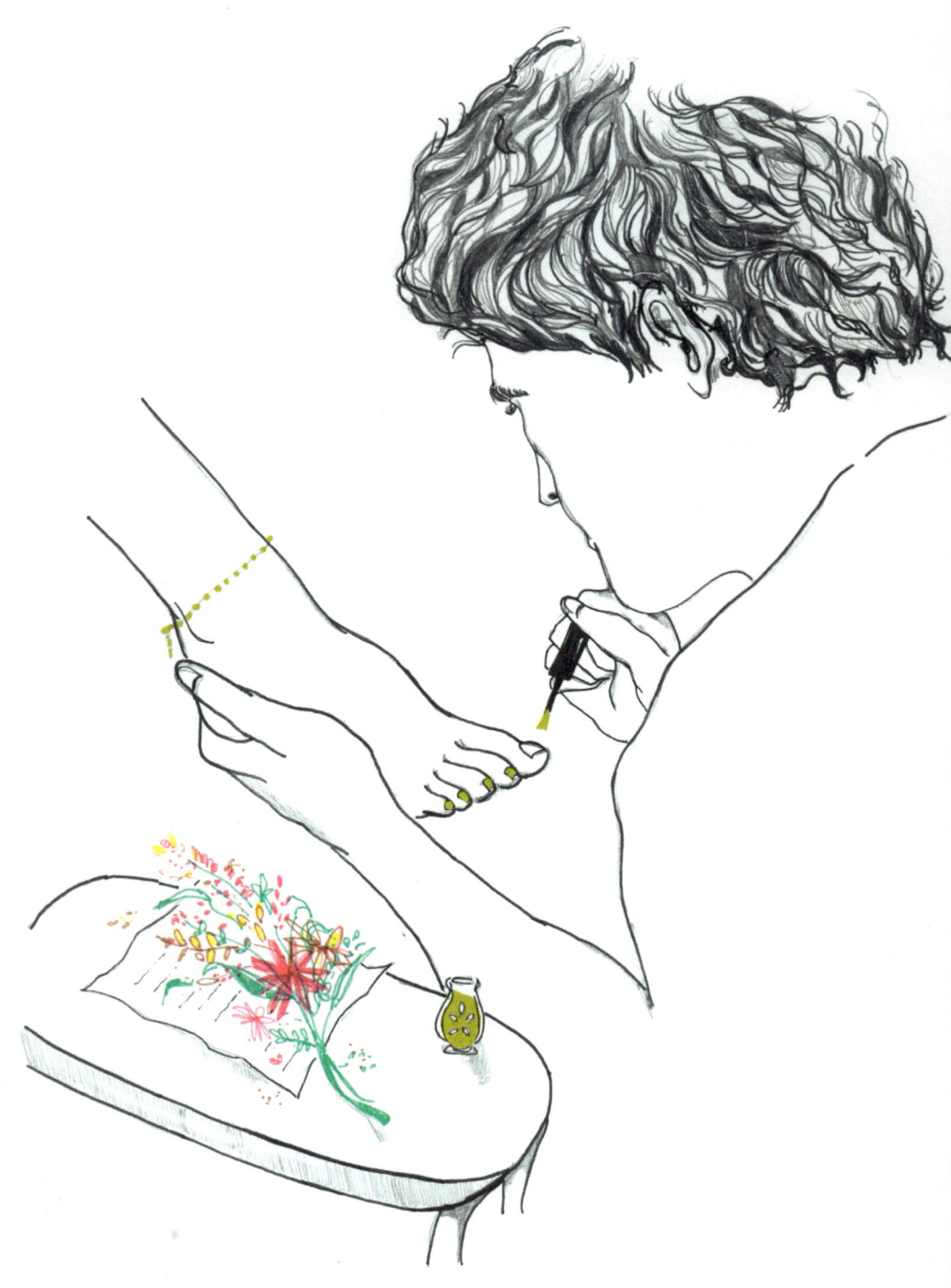

# The Ritual Part B: Painting Toes

He takes the heel of
my foot, cups it into
center of his palm.
Connects to callous, rough
skin.

He examines my size seven foot.
Soft lips kiss parched toes,
then he rests
foot on the bed.

In his left hand, he takes
"Gold Beam" nail polish
and brushes color from pinky
toe to big toe, careful to
brighten only nails, cuticles have no
smudge.

He purses lips and blows
on the golden colored toes as if
he's trying to put the flame out.

Paint flickers and glitters in
the reflection of his eyes.
Are we even this intimate
when we make love?

# Translations

I went to give him something solid,
mouth open with lips an inch thick,
wide tongue. The only physical piece
of me that can translate an emotion
I do not even know the name of.
Perhaps in Japanese or Cantonese,
or maybe even in Arabic, they have
a word or pitch for this feeling.

Maybe if I had the word I wouldn't
press down firmly onto his chest -
index fingers that twirl dark hair would
interpret pronunciation and ideas instead.

Tanned inner thighs wrap around hips,
as if that place is carved just
for him, could instead be a gesture
of downcast eyes, long eyelashes curled
ever so slightly would be the only
innuendo for this position.

Just maybe I wouldn't literally lose
an inhalation of breath each moment
I feel him inside of me. Not just
a gasp or sigh either, but a lung full
of air. Where I go to different elevations
and my definition of sex changes.

I wouldn't feel 210 pounds
of pure man pull me deeper into *him*
and lose sense of what I am feeling,
overpowered by testosterone and
absorbed into his ecstasy.

What word do they have for that?
Or is this only an Eastern monk's
meditation,
a place of enlightenment?

Can I really blame
my lack of creative expression
on the English language? Can I
really believe that if I was a linguist
I would rather mumble a word to him
than briefly shudder every time
I see these finger-marked bruises
on my inner thighs?
Feel hormones of heightened estrogen
that want him to grab me harder.
And he does
without downcast eyes or
words of sliding pitch.

# Emotional Space Equals Logic

**emotional**
I am swimming into him, like there is nothing else to me.

**space =**
All of a sudden there is a segment of hangers for his XL t-shirts in my closet. There is a space on the kitchen counter reserved for his books. The end table is pushed aside in the living room at a certain angle so we can sit side by side. The pillow next to mine is not two inches fluffier anymore.

**logic**
I pretended I was asleep when I heard those three words. The words you hear that are a heartbeat all on their own. I … Love … You … I think my body may have jolted a certain way, breathing pattern got a little erratic. You know, I instantly became confused and felt that electricity they call phenylethylamine jolts mind and body. It stirred me up so much I think I actually stopped breathing for a minute and then was instantly gulping air. It's like the oxygen cut off to my brain was a reason not to respond. Because what do you say to something like those three words, except those three words back. But, I think I pulled it off. I don't think he knew I heard his audible heartbeat at four in the morning.

# 18 Hours

**1 a.m.**
His rough hands
cup my hips, a
little lower, as if
his grip makes me
grow wider, spreads
my wings, and I
metamorphosize.
He gathers pollen.
"I forgot how incredible
that was," he sighs,
his tongue
wets my skin.

**7 a.m.**
"I don't want to hurt you,"
he says, "but there is
somebody else."

**9 a.m.**
Don't get weird on me,
he IM's me.
I think of the options I have:
1) tell him to fuck off
2) play with him
3) try to be friends
4) remember I'm married

**7 p.m.**
I'm living off
memories of his climax.
The way he said
my name, the way
I had a mental orgasm
that flexed my naval,
the way he smoothed
my wings.

# Washed by Hand

There is no extra time for ironing
long-sleeved shirts; careful around
buttons.
My skin feels wrinkles that won't fade
without your touch — your scent.

Just because it's July, time for thin
sundresses
that have no buttons, does not mean
grass cannot imprint designs on clothes,
skin.

I would trickle back time on your clock
so you would unbutton me,
not just my clothes.

# Dreaming in Spanish

His wet tongue smoothly traces
cervical nerves over delicate neck,
He breathes deeply in Spanish.
Inhales known skin, opens Cuban
lips a little wider,
bites slightly.

He was in my dreams … again.
291 nights later I can still feel him;
hard. Warmth shaped like a spoon
where I fill him up overfull spilling
onto memories of what I never knew was
love until I awake 291 nights later to
finally cup in my hands the perpetual
question, "Why does he reverberate in my
cerebral reality?"

My body is vibrating, tingling with
reminiscences
of the first kiss, pins and needles
shocking my cells
like an electrical cord sparking from a
sprinkle of water.
Yet, our last kiss was nearly a year ago.

I can't shed him. My skin has been
replaced nine times, but
I still feel his large, rough hands cradle
my hips, tipping me
back towards him. My blood cells have
been renovated two and a half times,
but I have stopped bleeding.
Stopped dreaming of nothing but him.

This is no longer a fleeting thought,
or a faint remembrance of a dream
that hits reality like déjà vu, but is
forgotten quickly. Only a subconscious
memory tied up in dendritic spider-
webbed shaped
thoughts in the cranium.
No, I was actually holding
onto this thought.

Cupped in my hands. Could see it, smell
it, feel it, know it.
Skin that lasts longer than déjà vu.
Had my epiphany.

# Insomnia

I'm tucked away in a space
writing to forget you.
It's been a good nine months
and I can finally feel the
rounding of this pen materialize
more of you.

For three months, I couldn't even
use a keyboard to type your name,
couldn't live 500 miles close to you,
couldn't have a phone with your
number in it. My subconscious mind
was my enemy as you snuck into
my REM moments every night.
I stopped sleeping. Then you crawled
into my insomniac mind 24 hours a day.
I took sleeping pills and only had a
vague scent of you when I woke up,
soaking wet.

"It just takes time," they said, and nine
months later my cerebral life is no longer
saturated with cells strictly named
after you.

# Lexapro and Chocolate

You seem like 10 lives ago,
but it has been less than a year.
I've collected over 30 numbers in the
past 10 months but haven't returned
one call. Have become a mute in
possible relationships and gained 10 pounds.
I've replaced sex with chocolate and
birth control with Lexapro.

Double dose
Double fudge
Double digits

I can't answer a phone call,
as I have no words to softly murmur
since you aren't here to receive them during dark nights.
Instead, I manifest a Rubenesque physique
and curl up into each curve.
My own insulated hammock.
And I am only 28 - but
these people surrounding me keep wishing
marriage on me.
I found my first wrinkle.
Gravity is settling, yet I have lived
10 lives in 10 months, had 30 offers,
gained 10 pounds of comfort.
Traded estrogen for serotonin.

# PART II

*On family love that bonds the deepest*

# Our Habit

We lay on Easter day, side by side
on a Mexican blanket, fanned out in a field
sprinkled with pine trees hiding the city.
Four years ago, we faced each other
on a cobblestone wall
that divided ocean and land,
moon and sun.
We knew silent magic
would be added each year.
Words, not necessary for potion,
were never a secret ingredient.
Only when we sit alone, knees inches from touching,
does atmosphere stir into a peace that is whole,
that makes us evaporate
into earth or air.
We mold into soft dirt of field,
hips rounding into clay bed,
where dew will gather when this day is over.
Pastel greens, pinks, blues of blanked and clothes
are no coincidence, almost a Monet
where colors drain into others;
we breathe in pine tree's sighs.
Another year will gradually revolve
like our canopy of clouds.
But our knees will try to touch again, next spring.
Ritual so tight, it has become tradition.

# Grandma Rustic(k)

1
Isabel Rustick, my Hungarian grandmother
gently traced intricate mazes
with long, pointed fingertips
on my tightly woven palms.

Experienced index fingers
and thumbs of dough
breaded my mind
with fairy tales of ancient genealogy.

Breath of iris escaped Grandma's
painted crimson lips of petals, tickling
nerve endings
rooted within the deep tissue of my thoughts;
stimulated quiet imagination.

Olive green flesh matched mine,
except for virgin rivers of veins,
rushed whispers and tumbled
over knuckles clumsily, exposing infant truth.

2
Multi-colored Buddha sat yoga style,
centered in exotic flowers, shaped semi-circle, in the far back yard.
Grandma said it would protect
her, act as thick eyelashes that cleanse
sore eyes and flirt when painted.

Cranberry red licked the stone's
outermost layer,
mimicking Grandma's lipstick
as did the eccentric dyes which showed
their faded era in wrinkling places.

I wondered how many times she shook
off green gardening gloves of routine
and shut Buddha's eyes, with creased fingers;
dry paint fertilizing soil of foreign flowers.

She bathed him in colors of superstition
and took sharp scissors to hearty
neighbors who put their arm around
Buddha, trying to wake him.

3
Isabel knitted, with blue yarn,
miniature socks that would keep heritage
warm and worn. Strung up in a hammock
of placenta, he struggled.
Socks unraveled.

I, too, knitted socks in vain, wearing
Grandma's blue jean bellbottoms
from the '60s.
Her stomach's terrain no longer tucked
smooth but like rings in the core of trees,
folds breath female perfume.

Tight bellbottoms on belly did not cover
toes. Denim, not soft as yarn stitched
from her hands of fragrant lotion; no
longer did jeans press softly
over lower abdomen.
Bellbottoms jeans now unraveled,
blue yarn bleeds in my cells.
Her X-chromosome socks
made me rustic(k).

# Isabel, the First

Japanese angled face, high
cheekbones with no apparent eyebrows,
Hungarian nose. You are my east —
with fortune cookies called whiskey
cookies and fortunes scribed deep
in my palm — reverberating throughout
my nervous system. I am spiraled around
your DNA. It twirls in molecules "Isabel"
throughout my body.
Whispering back to Habsburg Royalty.
We are a tribe of ancient days, yet our
language is changing... except in cells made
up of you.

# Monk Fetish

I think she's in love
with the Dalai Lama.
Not that she really believes
that he is the Ocean of Compassion
or really reincarnated, but I think
she's in love with the actual man.

I mean, we were there
at the 51-year annual protest.
Marched with Tibetans at the
government in exile's home.
We tasted Himalayan snow,
and heard mantras come from
the mouths of old women
on their way to the market.

But she grew excited when
she held incense, prostrated in front
of His Holiness. I started to laugh
and whispered ever so softly
that he sounded like Kermit the Frog.
She grinned. Like two schoolgirls
we held hands, stifled giggles.
But, she had the crush.
Now she doesn't buy anything
Chinese, or at least says she
doesn't, with the exception of
the China Airlines ticket home.
At Christmas, she even drove
to 20 different malls, as if practicing
the Kalachakra*, trying to get away from
the 'Made in China' logo.

And how ironic it was that none of his
pictures turned out. A half of a monk's
head, a dark silhouette, and even the tape
recorder couldn't pick up his
high-pitched treble.
But, she still spreads those pictures out
and turns on the tape
and tells people that it really is him, and
they know she certainly is
in love with the Dalai Lama.

*Kalachakra: a circle made of sand and hours of manual labor by monks in the Tibetan Buddhist religion. It signifies impermanence and is destroyed once completed, and returned to the elements.*

# Grandfather's Tracks

He rounded hindquarters
of mahogany fur and
stroked downward with
stiff bristles.
Black leather strap
in large, tanned hands
brushed
belly, girth,
throat tenderly.
Dirt submitted to man,
and rushed
to cubicle floor.
He did this every day.
Day after day he followed
lines made fluent
by brush and fingers
to lead him to
America and out
of monarchy stampede.

"Take your horse,"
the trader dressed in
burlap said. And
he drove horse, son,
pride out of Transylvanian
hills, even though tarot cards
and gypsies pointed to danger
of frantic heels.

He mucked out
stall into open
Atlantic and
sprayed sweet lime
on wooden planks,
to keep horse tame
freshen molding straw.
Both Clydesdale and Hungarian
flexed muscular frame during the
groom, to feel control,
the instinct a musk scent for both.

This horse knew air strung of salt,
the measure of weight
a wooden wagon could hold,
the minutes a steeped
hill from a well.
It did not know
the sphere of the ocean,
or why men looked at hooves
with pick in hand when no
terrain was trotted over.
Why from bulb to heel
short, firm movements
were made.

Hoof to jawbone
is how he died
in a heap of lime scented
straw, with son to sell
horse, pride, name and
gypsies to claim
the tale their own.

# Anolu's Apples

*How Sarah's boyfriend deals with her anorexia/bulimia*

He peels apples for her.
This is a sacred act.
The chemist he is measures
each cut, slices away only
red, careful to leave the
fruit's meat in perfect proportion.

In the palm of this 25-year-old,
the fruit sits, untainted and whole
and he could toss its width like a
softball. But, he doesn't,
he holds it softly and
knows where it can
easily bruise. He feels
the delicacy of the pulp,
even through the thick layer
of waxed-skin on the
Washington Red Delicious.
Scrubs it softly and smells
her scent.

Even the act of buying apples
is like brushing his fingers
across her shoulders.
Spaghetti straps fall
inch by inch.

Each apple is studied and held
with a man's grip that
softens to calculate
curves and fullness. He
considers each one
as beautiful, but picks
only the immaculate ones, ones
that will bring more than
slight nutrients to her body.
This sacred act of alchemy
will nourish more than anorexia.

# Sarah Means Princess

Bones that protrude daringly through skin
do not make you Cinderella.
Hip bones pointed like stakes hold up a tent,
do not make an ideal home for womanhood.
Cinderella always had curvature
to cradle a laundry basket.
Where will your prince
find soft folds of skin
to cover him like a blanket,
when skin is shrunk to delicate frame?
Your hunger to be her will not keep
bone and skin fused.

I remember as children we had a puzzle
of Cinderella's transformation.
How many times did you try to shift
your seven-year-old body
into her three-inch frame?
You never understood the format, the fantasy;
will you ever see imperfections in her?
Now, you are on your way to treatment
for the seventh time, fed intravenously.
This time, I believe your fairy Godmother
will wand bulimia away,
replace it with Sarah
between bones and skin.

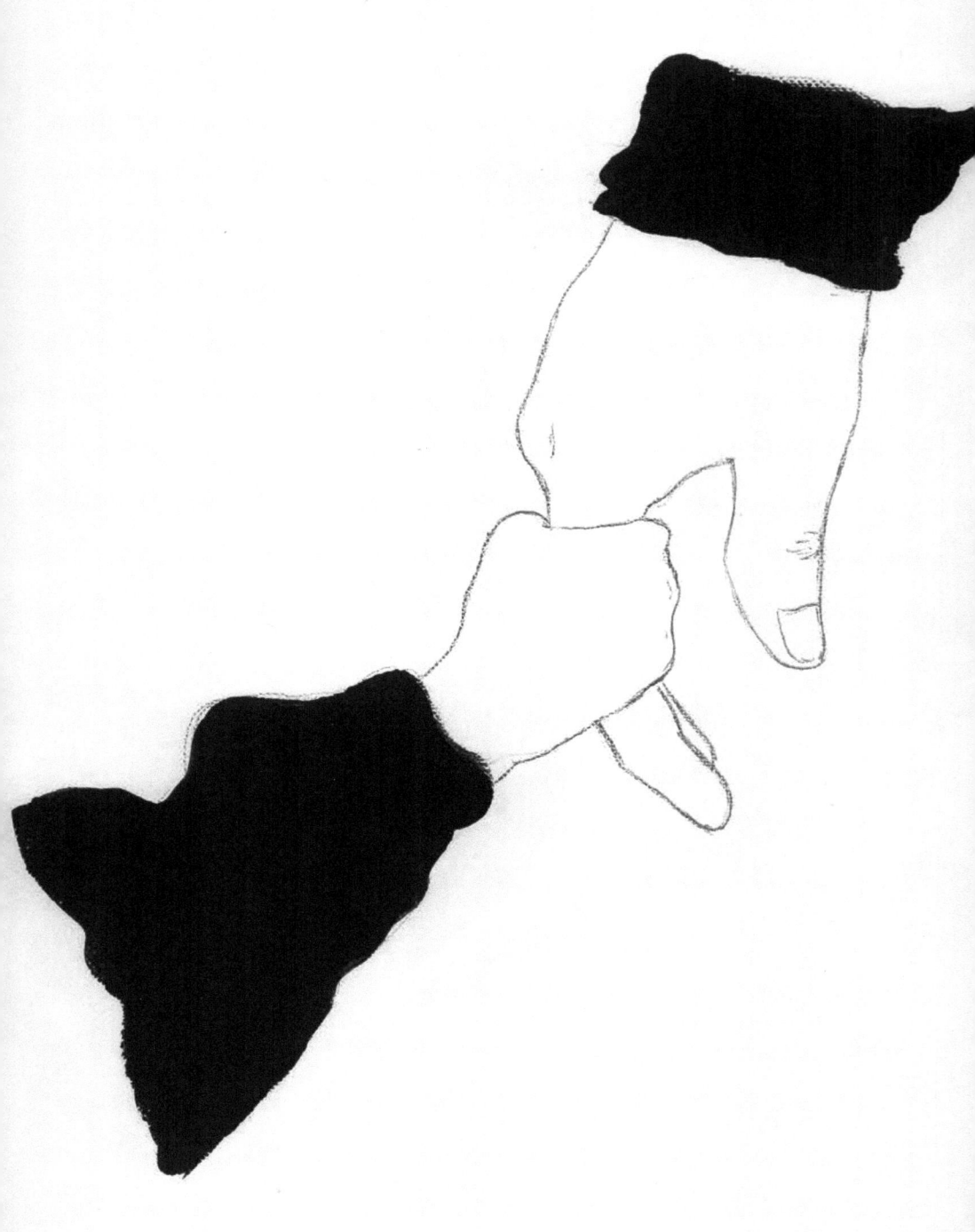

# Dad, Formerly Known as John

Long ago,
I was wounded.*
Two years old,
you were loudly ripped
out of my life,
like the last page
torn out
of a mystery
novel.
I cradled the
survival of that
book in
kindergarten;
drew crayon
pictures of everything
but you
in its pages during
elementary school;
built an altar of false dreams
for it in junior high;
shred it apart with
rebellious hands
in high school
and gave you the remains
of embarrassment
to edit in college.

We wrote
the final page
together, when
I called you 'Dad'
long-distance
and you
knew my voice
without introduction.

*opening sentence by Louise Gluck

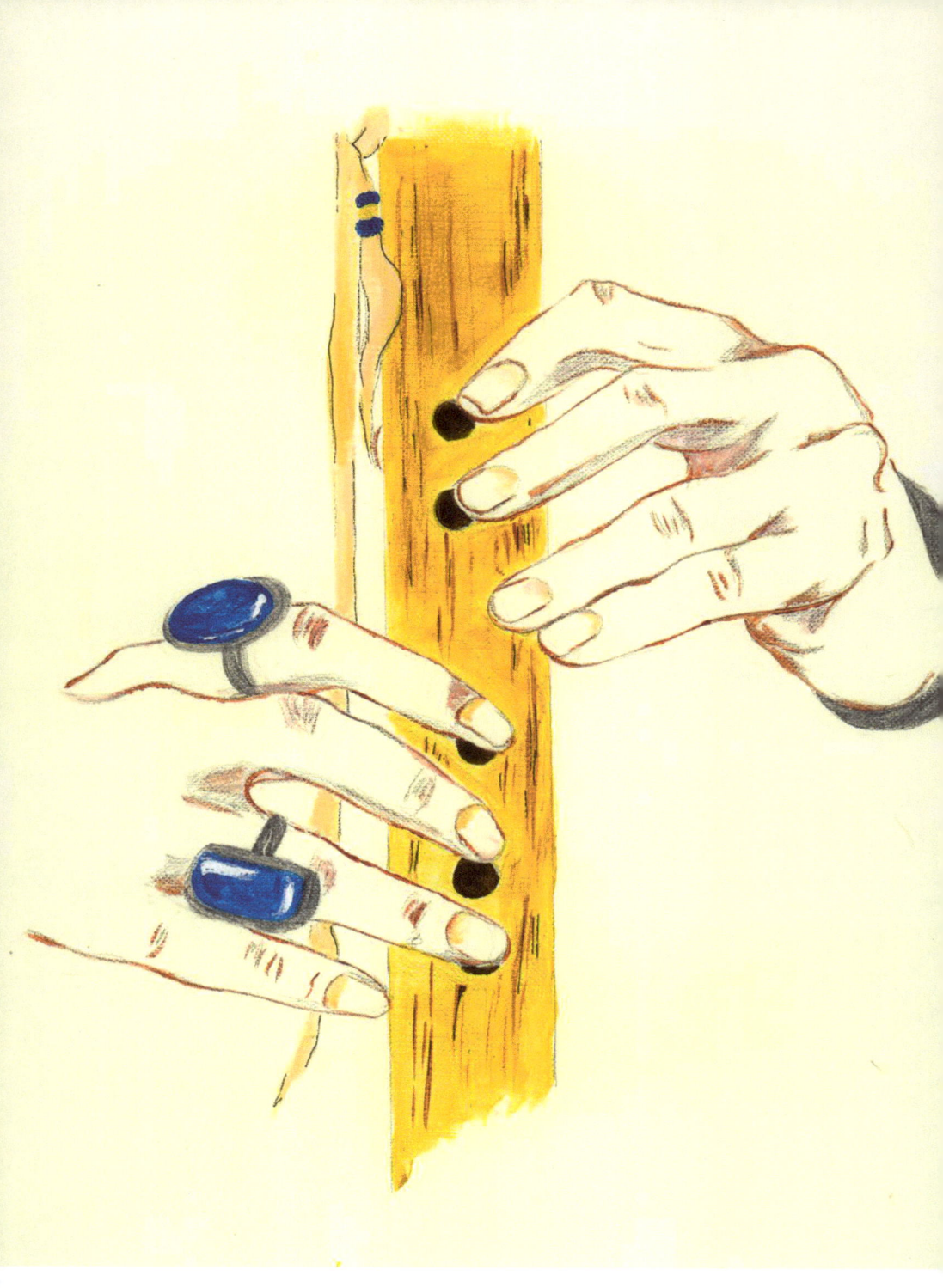

# Mema

This is my ex-husband's
red land and the sounds
of wooden flutes are his
words. I now know
what the notes F and A
say, deciphered they sing
mema.

Mema thinks I know
more than F and A,
and looks at me with
beady eyes, Indian wrinkles.
She cries when I leave
her small apartment
and those wrinkles
draw up, show me
how many rivers
she knows.

I cup hands, hold them
to light, try to convince
her red, Choctaw soil
does not wind its way
through my tissue.
I am not Sac-n-Fox, I
am not Pottawattamie.
She does not
stop crying.

"I love you,"
I say to a stranger,
I say to my ex-husband's
mema, I say to two notes I
still cannot play on
a wooden flute.

# Michigan Sandcastles

When I was young in Michigan,
home was a sandcastle
we sculpted with hands, sticks and rocks.
They were not made
with plastic shovels
or symmetric pails,
but our homes were not rounded smooth
and complete either.
We sifted dirt through small hands on
Lake Superior.
Just like our homes, though,
castles drowned with waves of
aggression,
formed new foundation.

My mother took us on figure eight paths
in the upper peninsula for years.
Lake to lake, home to home,
we always ended up barefoot
back by the water.
One summer she found us a home
on an empty bay
and we were washed free.
In our tent was room to tuck together
warm, safely away from the tide.

My brother, sister and I
learned our walls
were deciduous forests
and the lake which fell away to Canada
beyond our sight
was the horizon.

Our paintings were evergreens,
desert-colored cliffs
and soft aqua waves.
Driftwood, the motion of sun
and seagulls were our television.
Mom read books at night
around the campfire;
more than one bear cub
found comfort in those tales.

Our sandcastles were made
of more than sand, mud and hope.
We realized that even in August,
water can numb bare feet,
freeze an innocent world.
But we never gave up.
We were young in Michigan
and sang lullabies to the tide,
found home
buried beneath mud.

# Memories

Gold-rimmed leaves crackle
under Timberland boots in September.
I stroll down a hidden trail blazed
in rich chestnut and copper.
In my memory, I see colors that adorn
temples In Thailand.

Stars that drape the sky like tinsel
speckles a tree in December is what
my brother always studied.
He never had plastic, glow-in-the-dark
symmetric shapes which fade
as night drones on, but he kept
curtains fanned open, stretched like
his eyelids to wait in anticipation for a
bold star to take a
kamikaze dive into atmosphere.

This is land of Indian dance
where moccasins meet red ground,
spiral to the life of drums. The swirl
of motion chants throughout Oklahoma,
sound stomps and twists into dust,
creates a ghost to swallow land
and a war cry named tornado.

These years are not unlike snowflakes
that skate on wind to wool scarfs, mittens
and hats to be absorbed once again. This
snow is not willing to just land on a
child's tongue to be savored in a giggle.

In Tikal, Guatemala we climb mysterious
stone structures with small steps of steep
incline which turn into ladders and
tightropes the closer we came to the
canopy. We pass
symbols and art carved into rock,
natural as a river
snakes a ravine into mountain, this tribal
writing cannot be deciphered when
sweaty index fingers can't clear away
soot in wells made by time.

We continue past howler monkeys
who swing with gymnast charm and
screech secrets with emotion,
but we do not know this language.

We reach sun-hat sized leaves which
produce soft shade and illuminate
the rainforest around us in
safety; warn us not to break the canopy.

# PART III

*On internal longing for connection*

# India's Eyes

I cannot remain small in India.
Literally 1,860,000 eyes stare
at me. Eyes shaped from the wax
to the wane of the moon swallow
my skin.

My ex-husband has not even
studied me in such detail.
Not even my mother who mirrored
my face for hours when
my mouth was to her nipple.

Every blemish feels investigated,
every wrinkle magnified,
every scar traced, and
I cannot remain small in India.

I sit on buses, trains
and white skin pours over
onto cracked seats, meets
people on either side.
I cannot keep myself
proportional to my skeleton.

I do not tuck together
like the women
in sari's, wrapped so perfect
they resemble infants
folded in blankets. I fall
pant leg over pant attached
to a neon yellow backpack. Even
its vibrant color dulls next to India
and the Himroo fabric draped over Her
shoulder. Yet, 1,860,000 eyes
still stare not ready to spit me out.

# Mantra

Like a gondola meanders
through canals past crumbling
stone history, I navigate to you.
Redeemer, Jesus, God
have all held your English
name but I refuse to spell
you, vocalize your name
with only syllables
and tone.

I am out of the city
at a reservoir to give alms.
A September breath ripples
your dialect across water,
enchants like an Egyptian
belly dance.
There are hoofed tracks
in moist sand that tread
to shore. Is this how your
name is spelled? I investigate,
reach to the only mark a fawn
will leave during its morning drink,
follow ridges in the tear-shaped print.

Dirt crumbles into millions
of microscopic stones, blends
back into itself, disintegrates
shape. I try to find the holistic view.

The beach swirls with shades
of auburn and beige reminds
of Michigan's autumn
when white tailed deer
and dandelion spider dominate.
There is space here to prostrate
onto ground, leave imprint
that resembles a snow angel.

The sketch of the reservoir
juts out in strange directions
not like a cookie cutter pattern,
but dynamic like eroded borders
of the Soviet States, where
your September wind will reach
tongues and syllables in a mantra
not pronounced in books
I have read.

# Howl Poem

I have seen the most neurotic women of my generation, who all seem to keep an erect cup size 36C,
even at three in the morning,
when snoring softly on their backs.

Who are really brunettes
that have golden streaks of hair
in February.

Who wore Jordache jeans
and jean jackets in the 1980s
and sprayed aerosol hairspray in
highlights, resembling peacocks.

Who now wear low-riding Abercrombie and Fitch jeans exposing ironed bellies
that wrinkle into little balloons
at the end of the night when jeans are stripped off.

Who know the shakes from ephedrine and are so glad that guarana is still legal.

Who drink coffee in the middle of the afternoon for satiating hunger, yet are unable to yield a Big Mac in hands at nine at night.

Who glance sideways at windows of cars to check their reflection,
but only catch their mirrored image on half rolled up windows
to see their headless torso drifting.

Who know that Women's Tylenol is a diuretic and corrupt the minimum dosage to take five a day for the entire month.

Who drink cold water, instead of warm, to speed up the metabolic system.

Who purse collagen injected lips into soft pink puckers and smooth wide, red tongues over pinkness when they feel the eyes of a male — any male — hovering eyes on them.

Who every two weeks pay for sharp plastic to divide acrylic nails from organic nails and wince as they see blood speckle the Vietnamese lady's tissue who will receive $35 for the ritual.

Who always say, "no mayo, no cheese, no salt" before they choose what they want at a restaurant.

Who cut Hershey kisses into fours so they can enjoy one kiss for 12.5 minutes and then the next day tell all the girls how fat they feel from splurging the night before.

Who notice they're gaining weight when their outie belly button turns into an innie.

Who study other women's jiggles until the rumbling of their stomach
goes away, this can last for hours.

Who work out twice a day, seven days a week to take off one more pound.

Who take two hours and fifteen minutes in the grocery store for eight items because they weigh the pros and cons of less fat/more sodium, less carbs/more sugar until they walk out with only three items.

Who will nestle faded butterfly tattoos in cocooned wrinkled skin at age 68, yet still have erect cup size 36C.

Who foolishly think that a man will notice any of this.

# Apt. #4

These walls have remained
blank for nine months,
but I cannot make
them invisible.

I cannot dress them
in fine portraits or paintings
of someone else or
something else.

I tried to personalize them
by hanging photographs
of last year's vacation to Mexico
in rectangular spaces.

They were meant to bring
a touch of nostalgia,
but I became absorbed in
bright colorful dresses
on mountain tops in Creel.

I would smell scents
I do not know names of,
they became secret recipes,
spices for my mind.

Memories would not fade
but sculpted grooves
deep into the cerebellum
and I could not remain in the present.

I had to splash water onto walls
that held no taste or smell or sight,
but diluted impulses
to leave Oklahoma.

# Sediments

1
Earth worn smooth,
warmed by sun
has always held comfort.
Even when water rounds rock,
spills gentle song,
it seems silent.

2
I've put my hands
on top of Aztec hands
on ruins in Palenque.
I wondered why my hands
fit snugly on petite shapes,
why walls breathed heat.

3
I have seen sharp edges
from the Berlin Wall,
felt their cold, rugged remnants,
thought what rocks can do.

# Pacifica

The moon,
visible through
misted sea spray,
sparkles light
on palm trees.
The ocean's
whisper calls
me to the shore,
where I watch
white crests
surge upon waves.
Night angels dance
to the same rhythm.
Sea and sky,
like a mural,
drift and kiss.
I alone witness
the sea and sky
making love.

# Blue Moon Poet

I met Robert Pinsky when the moon
was blue.
The educated audience, a collage of suits
and ties, blue jeans and sandals, buckled
together forming fabric called crowd.
I tightened eyes to see in the auditorium,
crushed bones on pen and became
like a knot in wood yearning for texture.
Pinsky's quotable voice came
right out of books resurrecting life,
but after 10 p.m., when the crowd's tweed
tore and only a few procrastinating book
buyers dangled,
I heard the quotable,
"I only write when it's inconvenient."
Sunken empty bowls were under his eyes,
and I wondered where he would find
sleep to fill those
bowls tonight in this strange city
beneath a blue moon.
I wanted to tell him this crowd's material
was not soft as sheets washed by his
wife's hands.
But, I only let him sign my book,
thanked him quickly,
and hoped convenience would find him.

# Hieroglyphics

Translations, deciphers, hieroglyphics …
We speak with this and other.
Other than you and me, but it is us.
Becomes us, becoming us. We
are being, becoming, rolling in this
language of consciousness.

Our pores are the physical
sense of receiving/giving, the
only thing I can give to you,
I can't even explain. Is this
only afferent and efferent relationships;
messages stretched out
with kinesthetic cells?

I am a body.

Is this some statement from
the nervous system, that got
translated wrong? The unconscious
hum of cells zipping back and forth
from the brain to a certain body limb
to the stimulus and back again. One
could say sodium and potassium
are the yin and yang of the body.

I am the brain.

A cortex, a big mushy sponge
that has thoughts. But who can put their
arms around these continuous ramblings
and images that defines my sentience? As
if I could capture a thought and pause,
something even more phantom than wind.
Just exactly what are thoughts and where
do they come from and vanish, only to
bar me in the past or future?
I am the spirit.

This is the dance, the art, the no-thought,
spontaneity. The prayer. Or is this just
the brain and body working together?

To not be the body I would have no
sensation. To not be the brain, I would
have no identity. To not be the spirit
would I truly be sentient?
Metaphysics.

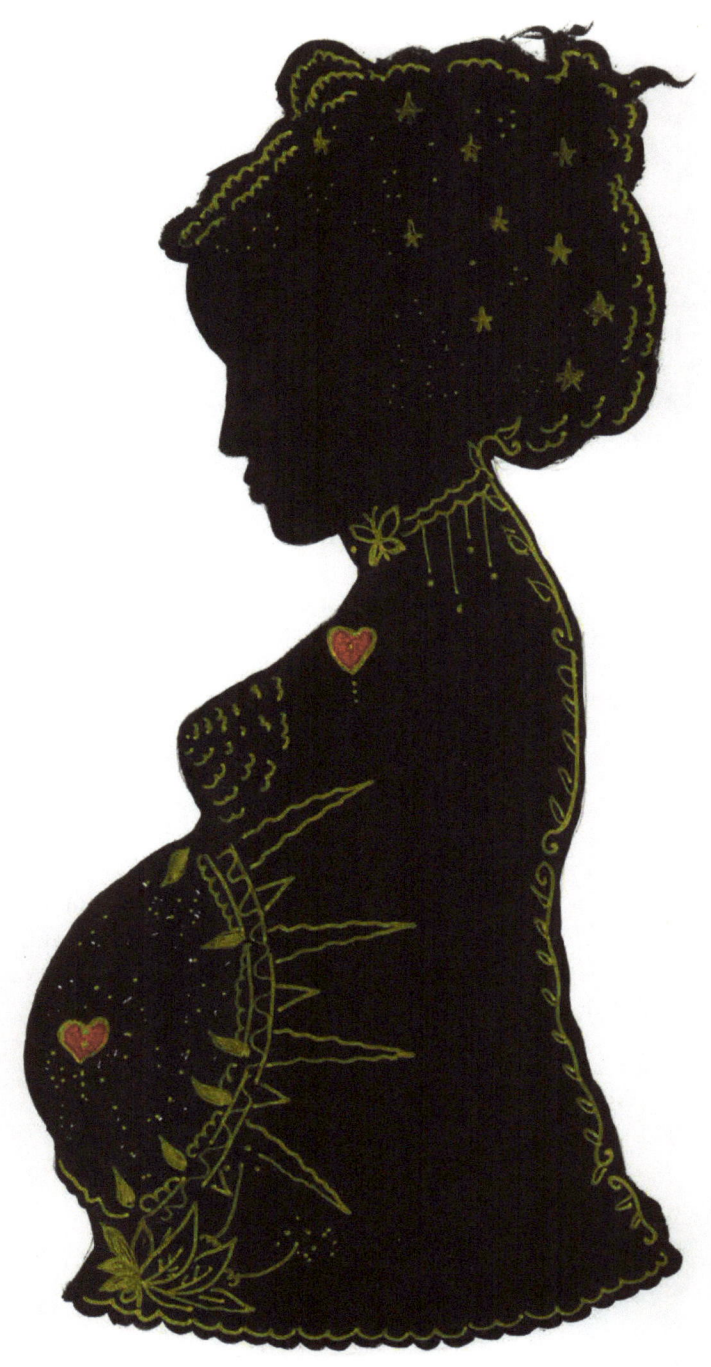

# Spirit Within

I put my hand on my belly
and try to find you.
I remember shooting stars.
I remember when I could
feel you in my veins,
belly had a heartbeat
of its own; supernatural
moved to natural.

And these organs
are messy, this skin
seems thick and unnecessary.

The contours in my mind
only seem fitting
to move from dimension
to dimension and grasp
what this breath
is made of.

And your proverbs
say this is only a temple,
what I always thought
was really me. I put
my hand on my belly,
and my mind travels
down organs and dimensions
and find myself a little bit more.

# Acknowledgements

I want to acknowledge my poetry teachers, Ms. Karen Holt, Marlene Bastian, and Eric Chock, for giving me a stage to present my emotions and to connect with others. I'd also like to acknowledge my high school crush, who never painted over a short poem I wrote on his bedroom wall. Thanks for giving me the courage to share my perception of the world.

Erica, xo

# About the Author

Sitting on the beach in her hometown in Guam, Erica Sand (aka Holly Rustick) dreams of possessing a superpower that allows her to create perfectly formatted novels just by thinking about them! But until that day comes, she'll have to contend with doing it the old-fashioned way.

When she's not daydreaming of new superpowers, you'll find Erica running a successful grant writing business and drawing upon her own exciting life experiences (from being an international expatriate to a fashion model to an award-winning press writer and a published poet) to create her juicy tales. She's also got a bad case of travel bugs having sojourned to over 20 countries. When not travelling, Erica adores drinking Pinot Noir and spending time with her gorgeous little girl – but not necessarily in that order.

Want to find out more? Visit her website www.ericasandauthor.com and find out about the Sojourning Soul Series.

Email: sojourningsoulseries@gmail.com
FB: @ericasandauthor
Instagram: @ericasandauthor

# About the Artist

Dorathina Herrero (b. 1985) is a painter, doll-maker and mother, born and raised on the island of Guam. She received her B.A. in Fine Arts, at the University of Guam in 2012, but developed a passion for the arts at the age of five.

She finds inspiration from within and around her — her works emulate the people in her life, her dreams and emotions. Her most current works may presumably be biographical, depicting her love for childhood, motherhood and love itself — all encompassing the island-life she lives.

There is a certain sensual sadness she cannot help but translate into her works, using her emotional and psychological unrest as motivation, which in turn grants her a harmonious fulfillment.

Her dolls and artwork can be found in the Guam Art Boutique in Chamorro Village and Bonita Baby in Hagatna, Guam.

Email: dorathina@gmail.com
Instagram: @miscmunekas
Facebook: @miscmunekas

# Quick Favor

Thank you so much for reading this book. I hope you enjoyed it.
May I ask a quick favor? Will you take a moment to leave
an honest review for this book on Amazon?
Reviews are the absolute best way to help others find out
about this book, and to know about related titles!

Also, I would LOVE to hear from you.
Please let me know what type of poetry you love!

Erica, xo

For more information about Erica Sand, visit:
Web: www.ericasandauthor.com
Email: sojourningsoulseries@gmail.com
Facebook: @ericasandauthor or @handfulofsmoke
Instagram: @ericasandauthor